Free the Children

How Red State Americans can Liberate Their Children from Government Schools

By James Ostrowski

Cazenovia Books

Buffalo, New York

LibertyMovement.org

Published by Cazenovia Books, Buffalo, New York

Printed in the United States of America

ISBN 978-0-9749253-7-0

First Edition

In Honor of

Murray N. Rothbard (1926-1995)

"The most erroneous assumption is to the effect that the aim of public education is to fill the young of the species with knowledge and awaken their intelligence, and so make them fit to discharge the duties of citizenship in an enlightened and independent manner. Nothing could be further from the truth. The aim of public education is not to spread enlightenment at all; it is simply to reduce as many individuals as possible to the same safe level, to breed and train a standardized citizenry, to put down dissent and originality. That is its aim in the United States, whatever the pretensions of politicians, pedagogues and other such mountebanks, and that is its aim everywhere else."

— H.L. Mencken

Contents

Foreword

I generally avoid urging people to engage in political action. I prefer direct citizen action as discussed in five of my previous books. Alas, strategy and tactics, while guided by theory, are ultimately pragmatic in nature and must be flexibly applied to concrete circumstances. Further, in battle, it is not advisable to inform the adversary that there are certain tools we will not use.

I can also rely on an old Latin legal maxim, *"exceptio probat regulam in casibus non exceptis"* (the exception confirms the rule in cases not excepted). In other words, the fact that an exception exists means that a general rule also exists."[1] This saying has a secondary meaning, that the exception *tests* the general rule. Both meanings apply here I suppose.

Direct action is to be preferred but there are times that call for *political* action and this is one of them.

Please note that portions of Chapters 1, 4 and 5 contain some material previously published in *Government Schools are Bad for Your Kids (2009)* and *Progressivism: A Primer (2014)*.

Thanks to Natalie Danelishen for designing the cover.

---

[1] Source: wordorigins.org.

Introduction

Since I published my book, *Government Schools Are Bad for Your Kids* in 2009, all subsequent events have confirmed my contentions. The schools have become even more oriented towards political propaganda and, as the country has moved left, so have the schools. Many of the products of these schools are floundering and often completely lost. They fill our prisons and jails but no one takes note.

Though there is an uptick in homeschooling, little else is being done about *America's biggest problem,* its K-12 government schools. The schools have become little more than a full employment scheme for overpaid Democratic Party activists and their *one trillion dollar budget* drains significant resources from Americans who now struggle to survive in a stagnant, progressive and locked-down economy.

Republicans have often complained that they cannot make major changes because the Democrats control this or that branch of the federal government or the Supreme Court might intervene. However, schools are entirely the creature of state governments, 23 of which are completely controlled by the Republicans. The Supreme Court has held there is no federal constitutional right to an education.[2] Table 1 below lists the 23 states controlled by Republicans that have *compulsory, socialist* schools funded by the taxpayers. Although Republicans claim to favor school "choice," 13 states they control have neither vouchers nor tax credits. Fortunately, 14 of the states allow citizens to directly change statutes and/or constitutions by petition and referendum. In those states, the citizens will have another option if the GOP-controlled legislatures refuse to act.

---

[2] *San Antonio Independent Sch. Dist. v. Rodriguez,* 411 U.S. 1, 35, 93 S. Ct. 1278, 36 L. Ed. 2d 16 (1973), reh'g denied, 411 U.S. 959, 93 S. Ct. 1919, 36 L. Ed. 2d 418 (1973); cf., C. Paulson, "Sixth Circuit Vacates Right-to-Literacy Ruling," sixthcircuitappellateblog.com (June 11, 2020).

Table No. 1

GOP States	Vouchers	Tax Credits	Initiative/ Referendum
Alabama		X	
Arizona			X
Arkansas	X		X
Florida	X	X	X
Georgia	X		
Idaho			X
Indiana			
Iowa			
Mississippi	X		X
Missouri			X
Montana			X
Nebraska			X
New Hampshire			
North Dakota			X
Ohio	X		X
Oklahoma	X		X
South Carolina		X	
Tennessee			
Texas			
Utah	X		X

GOP States	Vouchers	Tax Credits	Initiative/Referendum
West Virginia			
Wyoming			X
South Dakota		X	X

Republicans and conservatives constantly complain about the lack of school choice and the left-wing bent of teachers and their unions and the overall poor outcomes of the schools, but have somehow neglected to notice that they can simply *abolish the schools* in almost half the states without any interference from the Democrats. This book explicitly challenges them to do so and will challenge GOP voters in these states to pressure them to do so.

The GOP has not repealed any major aspect of progressive big government in a hundred years. See, Chapter 8, Table No. 2. This would give them a chance to prove that they take their own ideas and platforms seriously. If not, they might as well cease to exist as they likely will anyway, given present trends. *This is the one idea that might stop the trend towards a one-party left-progressive state in America.*

The book will also point out the prior uselessness of conservatism in all its branches and manifestations and will also challenge them to get on board yet another libertarian idea after decades of thwarting us.[3]

America is in a state of precipitous decline and in the midst of a rapid growth spurt in state power. The country has shifted from center-right in the Reagan years to the progressive left as a reaction to the election of the populist-nationalist Donald Trump in 2016. One of the major reasons for this is the progressive-left's almost complete domination of K-12 government schools. As I explained in *Government Schools Are Bad for Your Kids* (2009), these places are dominated by left-progressive teachers primarily associated with teachers' unions that donate heavily to the Democratic Party. Recent government school graduates voted heavily for Joe Biden over

---

[3] See, J. Ostrowski, *How to Revive the Liberty Movement and Defeat the Progressive State of America* (2019).

Trump, 65 to 31 percent,[4] easily supplying Biden with his narrow margin of victory—42,918 votes in three states.[5]

In my view, three main factors, K-12 schools, colleges and immigration have the country on the verge of permanent one-party rule by the left-progressive Democratic Party. There is a small window of opportunity to change this trajectory towards creeping totalitarianism before it is too late; before the opposition loses the political power to do so.

The problem of higher education is beyond the scope of this book, however, I will soon be rolling out a plan to push back against the accelerating trend of the left's domination of colleges.[6] Long story short, K-12 government schools manufacture state-loving progressives; colleges turn those kids into angry, hateful leftists. Hence, after many years of endless propaganda, many of our young people turn into robotic left-progressive Democrats.

Regardless of your views on "immigration," it cannot be denied that mass immigration is moving the country to the left. For example, Virginia, with the exception of the recent gubernatorial race, is now presumptively a blue state in large part because of immigration.[7] Immigration policy is also beyond the scope of this book. Suffice it to say I have elsewhere stated what I believe is the correct libertarian view of the subject. In brief, travel, movement, production and exchange are natural human rights; citizenship, voting and welfare are not. Alas, my "International Easy Pass" concept based on that distinction will likely horrify both the right and the left and is unlikely to be enacted anytime soon.[8] That being the case, mass immigration is likely to continue as the Democrats support it for obvious reasons and the GOP by and large supports it to cater to the wishes of its corporate donors for cheap labor. President Trump

[4] *Source:* NBC News exit poll (18-24 year olds).

[5] Calculation based on election results reported by Wikipedia. If Georgia, Arizona and Wisconsin flipped, there would have been a 269-269 tie with Trump likely winning in the House of Representatives.

[6] Follow LibertyMovement.org for updates.

[7] Matthew Continetti, "How States Like Virginia Go Blue (NationalReview.com, Nov. 9, 2019)

[8] J. Ostrowski, *supra.*

did briefly upset the applecart on immigration but even his policies did not significantly change the trajectory.

The intractability of immigration policy only serves to highlight the critical nature of the present project. There is also an interplay between government schools and immigration. If, on average, immigrants are more likely to vote Democratic and favor left-progressive policies, those tendencies are only enhanced when their children go to be brainwashed in left-progressive government schools.

This book proposes a bold but workable strategy to break the Democratic Party's stranglehold on our young people's education in a huge swath of the country.

1. Government Schools Are Bad for Your Kids

I wrote a book about it and will only summarize it here. See, *Government Schools Are Bad for Your Kids: What You Need to Know* (2009). This chapter summarizes the horrendous state of the schools at that time. Chapter 2 updates the situation in 2022.

Government schools were not established out of any dire need for them but rather for a variety of crass religious, political and economic motives. They were not immaculately conceived but rather were born out of a toxic stew of religious absolutism, Prussian militarism, utopian socialist leveling and special interest greed and power lust.

Today, government schools are loaded with crime, bullying, drugs and sexual promiscuity. They indoctrinate students into a false view of American history, one that is invariably favorable to ever-expanding government.

It is a myth that parents can escape to the suburbs to avoid exposing their children to school crime. A study by the Manhattan Institute found virtually equal rates of delinquency (drug use, pregnancy, fighting and theft) in suburban schools.[9] Government schools are unresponsive, self-serving bureaucracies that have to take eligible students even with criminal records, assuming they even know they have criminal records! They may even want to accept such students because they mean more state aid. Crime in government schools is in the nature of things. You get what you pay for.

Open and notorious and explicit sexual activity has also become a feature of daily life in government schools. Many government schools are turning into fornicatoriums featuring more and more sex, and less and less education.

---

[9] Jay P. Greene & Greg Forster, "Sex, Drugs, and Delinquency in Urban and Suburban Public Schools," *Manhattan Institute* (January 1, 2004).

Government Schools Are Bad for Your Kids

Moving on to drugs, your local government high school is often the best drug store in town. One suburban high school in Upstate New York is nicknamed "Heroin High." Government schools are the key distribution point for illegal drugs in many communities. One study concluded that "80% of the nation's high school students and 44% of middle-schoolers have personally seen illegal drugs used or sold and/or students drunk or high on the grounds of their schools."[10] Another study warns that rates of illegal drug use are no lower in suburban schools.[11]

Why is the problem so bad? Government schools are filled with people who don't want to be there and who are bored and alienated. As we are constantly reminded by those who *defend* government schools: they must take all students. The fact that your kids spend six hours a day with fellow students subject to virtually no screening process is hardly a recommendation. It is also difficult to discipline students. So doing involves a whole host of legal and bureaucratic procedures. In private schools, disruptive students can easily be expelled. In government schools, those in charge of student discipline are bureaucrats, not particularly responsive to parental or student concerns. Private school principals must be responsive or face closing their doors due to a lack of customers.

A word to the wise should be sufficient. If you send your child to a government school, they may learn more about chemistry than you could possibly imagine. As many as six percent of students in some government high schools are taking psychotropic drugs. Psychotropic drugs are powerful, mind-altering chemicals that can cause serious temporary and permanent side-effects. They are often given to bored students whose behavior disrupts classrooms. They are a method of control in a regime premised on control. The use of drugs to control students is the natural consequence of a system that forces parents to send their children to school and forces the children to be there. That's all the law can accomplish: guaranteeing *their physical presence*. It cannot guarantee they will show up ready to learn or be docile. That's where the drugs—chemical coercion—come in.

Sentencing your children to thirteen years in government school subjects them to running a gauntlet of endless assaults on their well-being.

---

[10] S. Boyles, "Parents Blind to Rising School Drug Use," WebMD Medical News (Aug. 16, 2007).
[11] P. Greene & Forster, *supra.*

Government Schools Are Bad for Your Kids

There is an epidemic of bullying in the government schools. In the extreme case, bullying can be related to school shootings such as Parkland. Nikolas Cruz was bullied at school. In fact, there is a video of it on You Tube.[12] It is commonplace to point out that many bullies are themselves victims of bullying who merely pass it along to those who are weaker since they can't strike back at the strong. The irony of the government school, the biggest bully of young people in America, urging its victims to stop being bullies, is completely lost on the bureaucrats.

Government schools are glorified daytime prisons operating in an atmosphere of legally-enforced nihilism which defaults into the pseudo-religion of hedonism. The hedonistic atmosphere of government schools is a necessary reflection of the nature of those schools. No reform is possible because such reform would make government schools the opposite of what they are: private schools.

As discussed in Chapter 4, the curriculum in government schools is laden with propaganda. It is critical for American citizens to understand their own history. However, they get a skewed view of history when the government controls the schools. A proper study of history must include alternative views and not simply the views that happen to be favored by the regime that controls the schools. Students should be given unimpeded access to information on controversial aspects of history and other subjects so they can learn how to think for themselves and reach their own conclusions.

I described the sad state of the country in 2009 as follows: "Currently, America is in a state of crisis caused by its global military empire, gigantic welfare state and the business cycle caused by the Federal Reserve. (On that evil institution, see Ron Paul's bestseller, *End the Fed*.) Yet, Americans are handicapped in dealing with these crises because few Americans know that the Federal Reserve causes a boom and bust cycle and that 9/11 was blowback for decades of Federal intervention into the Middle East. Thus, they fall for doomed policies such as Bush's War on Terror and Obama's bailout of the auto industry."

Worse yet, spending on government schools has established a permanent and large source of funding and workers for progressive Democratic causes. For example, Clarence, New York, is an affluent suburb outside of Buffalo where Republicans far outnumber

---

[12] "Video surfaces of Parkland suspected shooter fighting at school." https://youtu.be/WopGudVl6uI

Democrats. However, the Clarence Teachers Association is an affiliate of the New York State United Teachers and the American Federation of Teachers, both of which heavily bankroll Democratic candidates. Money flows from the taxpayers to the school district to the teachers to the unions to the Democratic Party. Thus, Republican parents who send their children to Clarence schools, are, in effect, bankrolling the treasury and ground troops of the party they vehemently oppose. To paraphrase Lenin, the capitalists are giving the progressives the rope they need to hang them.

America was supposed to be a highly decentralized peaceful commercial republic based on individual freedom and strictly limited government that minded its own business and stayed out of foreign conflicts. Instead, it is a highly centralized and militarized global empire whose extensive control over every aspect of our daily lives is rationalized by a distorted concept of majority rule that would have horrified the Founders—that majorities have a right to destroy individual liberty.

We have gone from a nation founded on loyalty to principles, including the right of revolution against tyranny, to one founded on loyalty to the government. Government schools are the foundation of big government in America.

The grand result of our experiment with government schools is a population ill-prepared to deal with the present crisis in America.

It is time to pull the plug while there is still a country worth saving.

2.   The Problem is Getting Worse Over Time

As bad as the schools were thirteen years ago, today, especially after the Lockdown, they are even worse.   Since *Government Schools* was published, several trends noted in the book have worsened.

In 2021, there were 31 school shootings, accelerating a pattern we have seen for many years.[13]   Some of the shooters are disgruntled students or former students who were bullied in government school. Bullying is "a feature, not a bug" of government schools. The entire enterprise is structured and designed to *bully* parents, taxpayers and students into attending and following orders. Bullied students, unable to challenge the system itself, pass along the bullying to those weaker than themselves.

The trend toward open sexual activity at school that I reported in 2009 is continuing and probably accelerating!   This headline is from 2020: "Students having sex on Santa Rosa County school grounds is growing problem."[14] In that fine school district, 41 students were disciplined in two years for apparently consensual sexual activity.

As with the other two of the big three government school malefactions—*crime, sex and drugs*—drug use at school also appears to be accelerating. One study concluded:

> "Arkansas, Nevada, and Arizona had the highest frequency of on-campus illegal drug use among high school students in 2017. In Oklahoma, the percentage of students using illegal drugs on school grounds between 2015 and 2017 rose by nearly 52 percent, and in South Carolina, that percentage increased by almost 17 percent over the same period. School districts in Chicago had the highest concentration of

---

[13] Source: Wikipedia.

[14] png.com (Feb. 5, 2020).

on-campus illegal substance use among high school teens in 2017 at nearly 1 in 3 students."[15]

Leftism has resurged in the last several years and so now, the *leftist* edict that we must ruthlessly and manically use the state to make everyone equal in every way has now been superimposed upon the pre-existing brainwashing in the schools, which has for many years inculcated the *progressive* belief that the state can and will solve all human problems using government force. The current combination of leftism and progressivism is a toxic stew poisoning the minds of our young people.

Critical race theory (CRT). There has been tremendous recent opposition to the teaching of critical race theory. This *is* an evil and false set of ideas and should be opposed. However, what many people fail to realize is that CRT is simply the latest wave of propaganda emitting from government schools since their founding in the 19th century. Government schools have *always* brain-washed and propagandized their inmates. That was always their original purpose. The nature of the propaganda varies over time and tends to reflect the intellectual fashions of the power elite that controls the schools. So, it is a great and good thing to oppose this particular instance of brainwashing of young people, but don't delude yourself into thinking that this one victory would cleanse the system. It won't. Only the complete shutdown of the machinery of propaganda— government schools—will save our children from left-progressive political brainwashing.

For a detailed discussion of critical race theory, see Chapter 4, below.

The militarization of schools continues at an accelerating rate. The largest district in the country, New York City, is increasing metal detector searches and hiring more cops.[16] If present trends continue, in a few more years, the prisonization of government schools will be nearly complete.

Finally, the Covid lockdown exposed the fact that the schools are run for the benefit of the teachers and administrators, not the students. Schools were closed long after this was necessary. Students

-----

[15] "High School Drug Use Across America," (Nov. 8, 2021) *project know.com.*

[16] A. Zimmerman, "NYC Adding More Metal Detectors and Police to Public Schools," thecity.nyc (Oct. 25, 2021).

were forced to wear masks of dubious scientific value. They were even forced to wear masks outside in hot weather and even during sports. There is a famous instance of a girl collapsing at the finish line of a race. All this cruelty was pointless but was supported by teachers, administrators, school boards and teachers' unions. These are the people parents entrust their children to seven hours a day, 180 days a year for thirteen years. It's time to say, enough is enough.

John and Nisha Whitehead brilliantly detailed what your children can expect to experience in government school these days: "From the moment a child enters one of the nation's 98,000 public schools to the moment he or she graduates, they will be exposed to a steady diet of:

- draconian zero tolerance policies that criminalize childish behavior,

- overreaching anti-bullying statutes that criminalize speech,

- school resource officers (police) tasked with disciplining and/or arresting so-called "disorderly" students,

- standardized testing that emphasizes rote answers over critical thinking,

- politically correct mindsets that teach young people to censor themselves and those around them,

- and extensive biometric and surveillance systems that, coupled with the rest, acclimate young people to a world in which they have no freedom of thought, speech or movement."[17]

On top of the long-standing cruelties and humiliations government school students have had to endure for some time, we

---

[17] "The Dangers of Going Back to School After a Year of COVID-19 Lockdowns," rutherford.org (Aug. 24, 2021).

can now add a lengthy list of Lockdown-related cruelties and indignities including some combination of mandatory vaccines, masks, distancing, plastic or glass partitions, isolation and quarantine, sudden cessation of in-person learning, temperature checks, ankle monitoring for athletes, restrictions on or termination of sports and extracurricular activities and intrusive testing. One must wonder how an institution that imposes such unfortunate restrictions without a scientific basis, can be trusted to teach *science*. The Whiteheads sum up the intolerable experience of today's school nicely:

> "Paradoxically, by the time you add in the lockdowns and active shooter drills, instead of making the schools safer, school officials have succeeded in creating an environment in which children are so traumatized that they suffer from post-traumatic stress disorder, nightmares, anxiety, mistrust of adults in authority, as well as feelings of anger, depression, humiliation, despair and delusion."[18]

Government schools *were* bad for your kids in 2009, are much worse now, and there is no reason to expect things to improve in the future.

---

[18] *Id.*

3. The Teachers Are Agents of the Democratic Party

Government school teachers form the base of the Democratic Party. They turn out to vote in high percentages. They donate large sums of money to candidates, both individually and in groups. In 2016, they donated $32 million and 94 percent went to Democrats.[19] One survey found that, of those who made political contributions, 83% of high school teachers donated to Democrats.[20] Finally, they actively volunteer for candidates. Their get-out-the-vote phone banks are legendary.

The reality is that Republican, Libertarian and Independent voters are forced to pay for this gargantuan group of Democratic activists whose lavish pay and benefits and part-time status, allow them to swing numerous close elections to the Democrats. *We are paying for our own political demise through government schools.* Aside from the welfare of our children, naked political survival and avoidance of a nasty one-party left-progressive state demand that we dismantle this institution immediately.

Teachers have the skills, the money and the leisure time to spend a great deal of time lobbying for bigger government across the board while we struggle to survive, juggling two and three jobs or side hustles and are too busy to oppose them.

Here is just a sample of teachers' salaries and pensions in Buffalo, New York. Over 300 teachers or other employees make over $100,000, double the average American's salary. 46 retired teachers or workers get a pension higher than $50,000, more than the average American makes each year. Of course, if you consider the wages of private sector, non-union workers, those paid purely on their worth in a free market, a mere $40,000, the disparity between the working class and political class widens even further.[21]

The salaries and pensions of teachers are truly enormous. Making supra-market wages and benefits provides them with the

---

[19] *Source:* Opensecrets.org.
[20] *Source:* Zippia.com.
[21] Source: Bureau of Labor Statistics.

motive to do political work and with the *means* to make donations so their candidates win while yours lose.

During the Lockdown, the teachers revealed their true nature: cheerleaders for creeping left-progressive totalitarianism. Beyond being good for your children, abolishing government schools in your state will drastically improve the overall political climate and push it heavily towards liberty.

4.   Your Kids Are Being Brainwashed, Not Educated

As stated in chapter 2, critical race theory is simply the latest form of political propaganda being foisted on young people in lieu of actual education.

As Isabel Paterson explained in *The God of the Machine*:

> "[E]very politically controlled educational system will inculcate the doctrine of state supremacy sooner or later, whether by the divine right of kings or the 'will of the people' in 'democracy.' Once the doctrine has been accepted, it becomes an almost superhuman task to break the stranglehold of the political power over the life of the citizen. It has had his body, property and mind in its clutches from infancy. An octopus would sooner release its prey."[22]

In a republic, the theory is that power proceeds from the people and the government is the people's agent and servant. However, when the government, through its control of the schools, is given the power to *shape the political mindset of its own citizens*, that master-servant relationship is turned upside down. *The government becomes the master, the citizen the servant,* first inside the classroom but eventually outside it too.

Professor Richard Ebeling brilliantly explains the propagandistic purpose of the government school:

> "Every generation of school-age children has imprinted upon it a politically correct ideology concerning America's past and the sanctity of the role of the state in society. Practically every child in the public school system learns that the 'robber barons' of the 19th century exploited the common working man; that unregulated capitalism needed to be

---

[22] *The God of the Machine* (New York: Putnam, 1943), pp. 257-58.

harnessed by enlightened government regulation in the Progressive era at the turn-of-the-century; that wild Wall Street speculation was a primary cause of the Great Depression; that only Franklin Roosevelt's New Deal saved America from catastrophe; and that American intervention in foreign wars has been necessary and inevitable, with the United States government required to be global leader and an occasional world policeman.

"Sometimes historic myths and ideological premises change. . . What is important is not merely the truth or validity of each of these facts, interpretations, or civic virtues. What is crucial is that they cumulatively represent the 'court history' and 'political correct' views that rationalize and justify a particular cultural ideology and a set of government policies and powers over society. They represent the official 'Party line' of contemporary American politics and culture that is taught in every public school. They legitimize the existing order of things and the particular political agenda of those who control the monopoly system of compulsory education. Whether we like to admit it or not, its function is essentially the same as it was in Soviet Russia, Fascist Italy, and Nazi Germany."[23]

In light of the obvious propaganda function of government schools, it must be emphasized that on a wide range of critical subjects, government schools would appear to be incapable of providing proper instruction at all! These include all the subjects where political philosophy plays an obvious role: history, civics, politics, law, ethics, and economics. Economist Ludwig von Mises believed it was "impossible to deal with any chapter of history without taking a definite stand on . . . implied economic doctrines."[24] He added, "The party that operates the schools is in a position to propagandize its tenets and to disparage those of other parties."[25]

---

[23] Sheldon Richman, *Separating School and State: How to Liberate America's Families* (1994), pp. xviii-xix.
[24] *Human Action: A Treatise on Economics* (Contemporary Books: Chicago, 3rd. Rev. ed., 1949) p. 877.
[25] *Id.*

Your Kids Are Being Brainwashed,
Not Educated

Additionally, there are various other subjects where politics can play a part such as health, science and literature. For example, since the power of government will expand tremendously if the public is convinced that we face a global warming crisis, will the contrary view get a fair hearing in the classroom? "Public schools . . . mold youth into loyal, compliant servants of the state," Sheldon Richman writes. "Their objectives have required a rigidity and authoritarianism that is inconsistent with the needs of a growing rational being seeking knowledge about the world."[26]

If it is the case that government schools are genetically incapable of honestly teaching a wide range of vital courses, a serious question must be raised about the value of the grades students receive in such courses. While a 99 in physics presumably means mastery of the truth about physics, what does a 99 in a government school American history course mean? That the student has mastered Propaganda 101? With respect to the ability to teach such courses, parents need to consider not only how government schools compare with private schools or homeschool, but whether government schools are capable of properly teaching them at all!

Not that there wasn't fair warning of all this. Early opponents of government schools predicted that governments would abuse their power over the schools for propaganda purposes. Herbert Spencer argued that, by its very nature, government schooling involves indoctrination:

> "For what is meant by saying that a government ought to educate the people? Why should they be educated? What is the education for? Clearly to fit the people for social life—to make them good citizens. And who is to say what are good citizens? The government: there is no other judge. And who is to say how these good citizens may be made? The government: there is no other judge. Hence the proposition is convertible into this—a government ought to mould children into good citizens, using its own discretion in settling what a good citizen is, and how the child may be moulded into one. It must first form for itself a definite conception of a pattern citizen; and having done this, must elaborate such

---

[26] *Separating School and State, supra* at 51.

system of discipline as seems best calculated to produce citizens after that pattern. This system of discipline it is bound to enforce to the uttermost."[27]

Critical race theory is the political propaganda *du jour.* Parents are right to oppose it, at least in its most virulent neo-Marxist form. Education at the elementary and high schools levels should focus on critical race *facts* as opposed to hotly disputed and highly controversial *theories* that are best studied at the college level.

Since there is no *precise* definition of CRT, lest I be accused of setting forth a straw man version of the theory, I will quote a prominent advocate with academic credentials. Professor Glenn Bracey[28], defined critical race theory as follows:

> "Critical race theory has six basic tenets. One is that race is socially constructed. Race is not natural. It is not biological. It is a social construction. It is not real objectively but it is real in its social effects because people put weight on it.

> "The second tenet is that race is a normal outcome of U. S. institutions and social relations. . . . Racism is the everyday operation of our American system. So, the fact that I wake up every morning in a black neighborhood is because of the history of institutional racism.

> "Intersectionality is the third tenet; it is the notion that our identities put us into different social locations. Those social locations come with specific needs and perspectives and insights on the world and that we can gain a lot about the notion of truth or the notion of how our entire society operates by paying attention to the people who speak from those different locations.

---

[27] *National Education* (1851).

[28] "What is Critical Race Theory, https://youtu.be/0G3UQlNvo-o (March 9, 2021) (at 5:13).

Your Kids Are Being Brainwashed,
Not Educated

"The fourth of course is the black white binaries. The notion that our society was largely organized along white on top, black on bottom; binary but that racism affects different racial groups differently so that native American are affected by race and racism differently than say, African Americans at some levels.

"The fifth and I would say most controversial is the notion that racism is permanent; that the racial poles of white on black are permanent and they're not permanent because of objective reasoning. They are not permanent because whites are superior to blacks or because blacks occupy some distinct role at the bottom. It's because whites are fixated on blackness and anti-blackness and they orient different other racial groups in the middle of white and black in order to protect their own superiority. In other words, racism is something that white people could decide to give up. They could change the social institutions. They could change their anti-blackness but they won't. Critical race theory recognizes choice but also recognizes a bit of permanence in that choice.

"And the last is a commitment to narrative. The law normally excises things it sees as extraneous but those extraneous things animate our racialized world and without them; without seeing how race contextualizes everything in our lives, we end up with fundamental injustices."

In turn, Professor Michael Rectenwald has summed up the numerous flaws in the theory:

"CRT essentializes race and those within races, figuring all white people as racist and all black people oppressed. It treats people not as individuals with individual motives and goals but strictly as members of their racial group. It denies individual agency to the very people it aims to liberate. It implies that racial group membership determines the beliefs and behaviors of those within said groups, curtailing an appreciation of their full humanity. It ascribes all outcomes to racial group membership, thereby denying merit to those in the "dominant" category (whites), while denying responsibility to those in the "subordinated" categories (blacks, indigenous, and people of color, or BIPOC). It makes contemporary white people guilty for the sins of long-dead white people who benefited from slavery. By incessantly harping on race, it exacerbates if it doesn't create racial strife. CRT is divisive and threatens the social order by provoking perpetual enmity between the races."[29]

He doesn't miss much. CRT combines some rather obvious insights with a large number of false or unproven ideological assertions rooted in neo-Marxism. It should not be taught in high schools as an indisputably true doctrine. It *is* a fit subject for college classes if subjected to a critical treatment (fat chance).

Aside from all its other flaws, perhaps the main problem with CRT is that, as a form of *scapegoating*, it misses the real villains in the tragic post-Civil War history of blacks in America. I recently published a monograph on this subject that I will briefly quote here.

"The problem of the black community is not white supremacy, it's government supremacy. After slavery, the government never got off the backs of the freed slaves and their descendants. Indeed, with each passing generation, additional government policies kept putting more and more roadblocks in the path of black people—Jim Crow, black codes, the racist policies of the Progressive Era, the discriminatory policies and huge taxes of the New Deal, the union and wage policies explicitly designed to hurt blacks in the job market; the war on drugs, which disproportionately hurt blacks systematically shut out of the economy and often leaving the drug trade as

---

[29] M. Rectenwald, "Vengeance and Sacrifice: Whiteness as Scapegoat in Critical Race Theory and Critical Whiteness Studies," mises.org (April 29, 2021).

their best option; the war on guns, explicitly designed to prevent blacks from protecting themselves from racist terrorist groups and from the government itself; the Great Society, which did what slavery failed to do, break up the black family—according to Jason Riley, "Only 16 percent of black families are married couples with children"; LBJ's Vietnam War, which hit blacks hard as they could not finagle their way around the draft, killing thousands and leaving tens of thousands addicted to heroin and doomed to a hopeless life when they returned to America; government schools, often explicitly created or operated on racist grounds to disadvantage black kids but forcing black taxpayers to pay for them anyway. Is there anything American government hasn't done to harm the black community? The freed slaves were never actually freed. They were never given the natural right to liberty that is the promise of America. In fact, things got worse and worse as time went on and government tyranny increased. The protests and riots of recent years are the result of a problem that was never addressed and frankly, not even well understood as left-progressives have monopolized the debate to cover up their own sins. The problem is not white supremacy but government supremacy over black people in America."[30]

CRT, instead of grasping and grappling with these facts, sets up a scapegoat that only results in distracting attention away from the real problem and cruelly stirring up race hatred which leads to the mindless violence we have seen since the Ferguson riots.

Even if parents spend tremendous effort defeating this false and destructive CRT curriculum, the left-progressive infrastructure that controls government schools will remain and will tirelessly inject similar leftist propaganda into the curriculum when you go back to your normal life.

---

[30] James Ostrowski, *Progressive Big Government's War on Black People* (1865-2021) (2021).

5.   The Schools Can't Be Reformed

The reaction of Republicans and conservatives to the endless failures of government schools has been *reformism*.   Why is the Republican or conservative constantly trying to make failed government programs work better?   I explained the failure of the progressive approach to policy and government in *Progressivism: A Primer (2014)*.   Progressivism fails due to its intrinsic nature.   It cannot be reformed. Anyone attempting to reform a failed progressive program is implicitly accepting the premise of progressivism, that centralized government force can improve society. It cannot. Don't reform. Abolish! Repeal! Eliminate! Repeal *and don't replace*. You don't need to replace force with other forms of force, even lesser amounts of force.   Replace force with liberty!   Let people figure out their own destiny.   That was the original American idea that created the greatest country in history for ordinary people, meaning people not part of the power structure. What is *my* plan for your life?   To let you choose your own plan!

Why the schools cannot be reformed is explained in detail in *Government Schools*.   No reform can change the nature of government as a coercive bureaucracy that exercises power over students and parents in an asymmetrical manner.   They control you; you don't control them.

Government schools are coercive institutions; private schools are voluntary. Due to compulsory school laws and laws making home schooling difficult, students whose parents cannot afford private schools and find homeschooling impractical must attend a government school. Taxpayers must pay for them.   The rules and regulations governing government schools are rigid, inflexible and by definition, coercive. The teachers unions gain great power over the schools by application of federal and state laws granting them special legal privileges. Throughout the bureaucracy, due to civil service and union rules and laws, it is difficult for anyone to be fired.   The schools must accept virtually all students whether they want them or not and whether or not they are fit for a classroom. Students and parents and even teachers who do not like the way the schools are run have few options for changing things. The main point is that relations among people in government schools are coercive and involuntary. Those with legal power tell those without legal power what to do. Those without power have little choice but to comply.

In the government school system, there is a hierarchy of legal power. Roughly speaking, that hierarchy starts with the state education bureaucracy and proceeds *downward* to local school boards, then to the superintendent, down to the principal, the teachers and finally, at the *bottom* of the pyramid, the students and their parents. On certain issues, the federal government sits at the top of the pyramid and can bark orders at even the state education departments. *It is a top-down, coercive, bureaucratic model of decision-making.*

What are the ramifications of such a structure of decision-making? Given the assumption of human self-interest, those with power tend to act in accordance with their own interests. They will of course rationalize this behavior by saying they are acting in the public interest or the student's interest. However, since they have unilateral power over those below them in the pyramid, they can make their decisions without consulting them. They can so act even if the students and the parents are absolutely positive that their decisions are not in their interest. *Their opinions simply do not matter.* They are mere bystanders.

In sharp contrast, private schools are voluntary institutions. While (non-home schooled) students must go to some school, they need not go to *that* school. And they can leave any time. The private school doesn't have to admit them and can, more or less, kick them out any time. The principal can, subject to contractual severance pay, be fired anytime, or leave any time. The same is true with teachers. Though there may be private school teachers' unions in some places, they do not have nearly the power of the government school unions to keep incompetent teachers on the job forever. Instead of being at the bottom of a pyramid of power, parents who send their children to private school are on a horizontal plane with the school, itself. *They are equal to one another in the power to sever the relationship.*

What are the ramifications of the voluntary nature of the private school? There, you can't merely *say or think* that your actions are beneficial to the other parties involved. They must actually be perceived as such by those parties. If not, they will walk away. The actions of the parents and students, the teachers and the administration must be mutually beneficial and perceived as such because no one can impose their will on the others for more than a very short period of time, say, till the next school year starts. *Everyone must be on their best behavior at all times and no one has the power to exploit the others.*

Power Flows Down

U. S. Department of Education
↓
State Education Department
↓
School Board
↓
Superintendent
↓
Principal
↓
Teachers
↓
Parents and Students

The chart above illustrates how *power* flows down in the government school system. It turns out that *information* travels in the same direction as power. All top-down bureaucracies share this fatal defect: *a shortage of valuable information flowing up to them from below.* If you sit at the bottom of a pyramid of power, there is little incentive to pass upward information about the defects of the system or suggestions for improvement. As economist Thomas Sowell explains:

> "Feedback which can be safely ignored by decision makers is not socially *effective* knowledge. Effective feedback does not mean the mere articulation of information, but the implicit transmission of others'

knowledge in the explicit form of effective incentives to the recipients."[31]

Private schools receive valuable feedback about their operations from students and parents who expect their complaints to be taken seriously because they have the option of going elsewhere. Government schools are starved of such "effective knowledge."

One way or another, all the defects of government schools described in this book arise out of the simple, fundamental and inescapable fact that government schools are top-down coercive bureaucracies while private schools are based on voluntary relations. As sociologist Rune Kvist Olsen puts it:

> "Hierarchies are, by their very nature, systems of domination, command and control. They are essentially systems and structures of institutionalized domination. They place people in ranks of superiors and inferiors. Positioning some people above others activates particular 'drives' or responses and *steering mechanisms* to arrange and legitimize someone's control over others. Researchers have noted that whenever control, coercion, use of submission and domination in the name of rank and position occurs, hostile and destructive forms of interpersonal relationships emerge."[32]

Thus, government schools are a coercive bureaucracy. School board elections have proven ineffective in allowing citizens to impose their will on these bureaucracies. Special interest groups dominate these elections even more so than is the case with elections generally. School boards are chosen in special elections with very low turnouts. Most of the voters have a special interest in the outcome, for example, school district employees and the parents of students. The general interests of average citizens are not a significant factor in these elections. The results are predictable: bloated payrolls and high taxes. Giving voters the right to approve budgets has utterly failed to restrain spending. Again, such elections are dominated by special

---

[31] *Knowledge and Decisions* (Basic Books: New York, 1980), p. 150.
[32] "Vertical to Horizontal: A New Workplace Reality," April 8, 2006. http://www.uncharted.ca/content/view/149/35/

interests which favor higher spending. On occasions when budgets are defeated, similar budgets are often re-submitted until the opposition is worn down.

The future of our children is too important to be left to the whims of unresponsive and irresponsible bureaucracies or elected officials beholden to special interest groups. Reform efforts have failed for many decades. Don't reform; abolish!

6. Red State Americans Should Pull the Plug on this Failed Experiment

Red State Americans continually complain about left-progressive policies and personalities most closely associated with the Democratic Party. Yet, they themselves support or at least tolerate the very institution that is the foundation of left-progressive politics in America, the K-12 government school. They complain about this institution constantly, about its hostility to religion, its distortion of history, and its endless propaganda in favor of every larger and more powerful and more centralized government. And yet, they themselves send their kids there, pay the taxes that support the system and fail or refuse to use their undeniable political power to rid this menace from their lives for good. "Physician, heal thyself." Chapters 7 and 10 outline a plan to do just that.

7. The Mechanics of Dismantling the System

Determining the right state of affairs in society, politics and economics is a matter of *principle*; transitioning away from a failed system is a matter of *practicality*. Sure, we could try to push the proverbial libertarian button and be rid of the whole system overnight. However, such a sudden change in policy after 150 years would not only be disruptive to settled expectations and habits of behavior, but would no doubt for the very same reason be politically unpopular. It took 150 years to build this system up. It may take a few years to dismantle it. But certain steps can be taken *immediately*, as outlined at points A, B and C, below.

A. Repeal constitutional provisions guaranteeing a "right" to education.

Education is not a right. That assertion is socialist gibberish. Alas, this notion found its way into virtually every state's constitution during the nineteenth century. These provisions need to be repealed immediately. Education is a *service*, not a right.[33] As a service, it requires an expenditure of labor and capital to produce. Thus, to maintain it is a right requires one to show that one has the right to conscript from other people the resources required to produce the service. Thus, the execution of this alleged right requires both *theft* and the *forced labor* of third parties. There is no right to steal or enslave.

The hallmark of a true right is *universality*; the right must be of such a nature that all humans can possess and enjoy the right at the same time and in the same way. Yet, the alleged right to education means that some people must pay for the education of specific other people. Thus, the *payers* don't themselves have the right to education as *they* don't get a free education; they must instead pay for the education of others. Instead of a *right,* they have a *duty* to provide the right to others. This isn't a system of universal rights but a system of grifting, robbing Peter to pay Paul. In contrast, it is easy to see how

---

[33] See, Jonathan Bain, "Healthcare should be seen as a service, not a right," *reflector-online.com* (Feb 6, 2017) (arguing that health care is not a right but a service).

every human can simultaneously have the right to life if others simply abstain from killing them. No positive duty is implied or required and thus no asymmetrical right versus duty relation is created.

There are several other problems with the concept of education as a right. If I have a *right*, I have an absolute right to *demand* that others respect my right. If my right is subject to the whim and discretion of third parties, it can hardly be consider a right. Yet, that is precisely the case with the alleged right to education. The student gets no more and no less of whatever kind, quality and quantity of education the government in any particular area wants to dole out and if you don't like it, you can lump it. A right totally controlled by others is not a *right* at all but a *privilege*.

What *is* education? If it cannot be precisely defined, how can it be a right? There is no generally accepted understanding of what education a child should receive. Should it be theoretical or practical, academic or occupational? Which student gets put into which category? Which students get into honors classes and based on what criteria?

Surely, we can all agree that education should impart an objective, scientific view of all subjects. Yet, many subjects feature differences of opinion and many subjects tend to be presented in a way that suits the self-interest of the educational institution, in this case, the state itself. This is the final nail in the coffin of the notion of a right to education: the virtual impossibility of students receiving an objective view of reality in any area of study that directly impacts on the powers, privileges and prerogatives of the state itself.

Experience shows that the state will present a biased and tendentious view of the following subjects: history, literature, civics, politics, law, ethics, economics and religion. See, *Government Schools Are Bad for Your Kids*, Chapter 6. Logic tells us that this will always be the case. Thus, I have shown that the state is *incapable* of providing students with the right to *education*, that is, to an objective, unbiased, education, on all these critical subjects.

Finally, if there was a right to education, compelling people to partake of this right is an absurdity as true education, as opposed to rote memorization, requires a willing student. Compulsory education is a contradiction in terms.

B. Repeal compulsory attendance laws.

Amending constitutions to delete the absurd nullity of the right to education will likely take a while. However, this step can be taken immediately. It will not only restore *the family* as the decision-maker on the education of their children but will provide the legal framework for allowing the free market to provide innovative education and school options and products without fear of violating arbitrary government regulations.

C. Repeal all regulations on private and religious schools and homeschooling.

Ending compulsory schooling necessarily entails repealing all regulations that allow alternatives to state schools but only under a lengthy set of conditions rigorously enforced. These include teacher certification and licensing, curriculum requirements, mandating the length of the school year and school day, record-keeping and reporting requirements and standardized testing requirements. Repealing these arbitrary rules and regulations will immediately reduce the cost of private education alternatives and will allow them the flexibility to serve the unique needs of students and families. These savings and the reduced taxes resulting from the phasing out of government schools, will make private education solutions much more affordable than they are now.

D. Create a tax credit for any family not using the schools.

This measure will put extra funds into the pockets of families to pay for alternative educational options including private or religious schools, homeschooling and even unschooling.

E. Grandfather-in existing students but reduce budgets and taxes on a pro rata basis as students leave the system.

Students already in the system and without easy alternatives should be allowed to complete their education undisturbed, however, as students flee the schools, budgets must be reduced accordingly and the funds returned to the rightful owners, the taxpayers.

The Mechanics of Dismantling the System

F. *Privatize school buildings and properties and provide <u>reparations for progressivism</u> to local residents.*

Again, property no longer used by the government must be returned to its true owners, the taxpayers. We must not allow funds from the sale of abandoned government schools to disappear into the bottomless pit of government budgets. Rather, they should be immediately returned to the local taxpayers. This will strengthen families and give them additional resources to educate their children.

G. *Close the system down after the last grandfathered-in students graduate from high school.*

Sell off the last of the real estate and make sure that all budget lines dedicated to school funding are returned to the people in the form of tax cuts.

8. The GOP Finally Has a Chance to Prove it is Not a Complete Fraud

For over 100 years, progressivism has been replacing the founding idea of America, individual liberty, with a different and completely opposite idea, that government force will bring us to the promise land. The counter-revolution started around 1913-14 with the introduction of the income tax, the Federal Reserve and the war on drugs (The Harrison Act). World War I was largely a progressive venture based on the notion that war would make the world safe for democracy. Before the War, the size of government spending had remained more or less steady for over 100 years with the exception of the Civil War years. However, government grew substantially during World War I and this growth, while declining somewhat after the war, never returned to its pre-war norm.

Starting with the War and continuing to this day, progressive big government would grow, as Professor Higgs has explained, in a ratchet-like manner.[34] Each crisis, real or imagined, would be used to justify major expansions in government size, scope or power. After the crisis was over, spending might decline somewhat but always remained larger than its pre-crisis level. Thus, various crises in the last 100 years caused a permanent increase in the size of government. These include World War I, the Depression, World War II, the Great Society and most recently, Covid19. Over the years, new, powerful and expensive government programs, agencies and departments have been created as dictated by the progressive notion that there is a government solution for every human problem. These include Social Security, public housing, Medicare, Medicaid, Obamacare and the Covid Lockdown and Bailout. See Table 2 below.

---

[34] Robert Higgs, *Crisis and Leviathan* (1987).

Table 2

Progressive Program	Year
Federal Reserve Act	1913
Income Tax	1913
Harrison Narcotics Act	1914
Minimum Wage	1933
Federal Public Housing	1933
Social Security	1935
National Labor Relations Act	1935
Federal Welfare	1935
Medicare	1965
Medicaid	1965
Department of Housing and Urban Development	1965
Department of Education	1979
Obamacare	2010
Covid Lockdown and Bailout	2020-2022

Although the GOP opposed many of these programs and policies initially, and even made some efforts to attack them when they were *out of power*, they made no serious efforts to do so when they held actual political power and over the years, even ceased their rhetorical opposition to them.

The GOP Finally Has a Chance to Prove it
is Not a Complete Fraud

The Republican Party platform (2016), makes various pronouncements about school choice including: "we will continue to fight for school choice until all parents can find good safe schools for their children." Typically, the platform appears to blame the federal government for the lack of choice at the state and local levels. This is a pseudo-explanation for the GOP failing to fulfill its promises or execute its alleged philosophy while remaining in power year after year. The platform fails to mention the obvious fact that they already have complete control over K-12 schools in 23 states! Will the GOP finally do the right thing and live up to its promises and rhetoric?

9. Will Conservatives Finally Conserve Something?

As I explained in *Progressivism: A Primer*, Chapter 6, the conservative movement has been a massive failure since its birthing during the Goldwater campaign of 1964. The movement has conserved nothing but left-progressive big government for 58 years in spite of its massive resources and political support and political victories.

Now, finally, here is an opportunity for the movement to change its fortunes. Instead of always working *against* the libertarians, conservatives could join forces with us to rid the nation of the failed progressive experiment of having the government raise our children (badly) from age 5 through 18, with ever greater pressure to lower the school age and expand school hours and even further estrange American families from their young children.

Government schools were *not* part of the American Founding[35] and contradict all of its main ideas. They are an attack on the family, an institution conservatives have always claimed to defend. It was and is a radical progressive and socialist experiment that failed.

I challenge conservatives and their movement to shake off almost six decades of miserable failure and finally do something to actually conserve things of value: the family, liberty, religion and the free market. Help us to free the children now!

---

[35] Benjamin Rush was an exception among the Founders who advocated for government schools.

10. What You Can Do to Light a Fire Under the GOP and Conservatism, Inc.

Lobbying for change is usually very hard. Your proposal may run into ideological, political or special interest group opposition. Success is never guaranteed but this effort starts out with some important, baked-in advantages. These 23 states are already controlled by one party whose stated philosophy and specific policy pronouncements are both favorable to this proposal. That is the whole point of this book and this movement. *Pick a fight on favorable battlefields where you control the high ground.*

Nevertheless, there *will* be strong opposition. There are vast and entrenched special interest groups that will oppose this proposal: the army of government school employees and contractors and current parents not willing to take responsibility for the education of the children they brought into the world. Moreover, you will be opposed by that segment of GOP officials who either don't really believe their own rhetoric—it was just to con the voters to win elections and maintain power—or those who do believe their own rhetoric but don't want to rock the boat and risk defeat in an election. Imagine the horror of losing an election and having to get a real job! Keep in mind that the re-election rate of state legislators in America is quite high—95%.[36] They do not win that frequently by rocking the boat but by playing it safe and keeping their heads down.

You may have to light a fire under state legislators to do the right thing. *Nothing focuses the mind of a politician like a surprise primary challenge!* So, early on in the process, even before any decision is made to run candidates, start to identify potential challengers. Look for solid citizens who have achieved success in their fields and who have the personalities and communication skills and economic independence to run for office. Potential candidates should take a lead in lobbying efforts so that if those efforts fail, they will already have attracted some notoriety among the press and public to provide a jump start to their campaigns.

Keep in mind the political class has constructed many barriers to newbies running for office: ballot access rules, arcane campaign

---

[36] *Source:* Ballotpedia.org.

45

finance regulations and financial disclosure laws. *Be sure to consult with a local lawyer for advice* on avoiding these traps and pitfalls *deliberately designed* to make your life more difficult.

It will be up to the citizens of each state to form their own organizations and formulate and execute their own strategies and tactics. Here, I can only provide the broad outlines of starting a true, grassroots movement.

1. Choose a state coordinator who has the time and energy to lead a movement for at least one year at which time, she can be replaced by another volunteer. Frequent rotation of volunteers is necessary to avoid burnout. Keep in mind that the political class we are fighting *never burns out* because, while you *burn* time, money and energy with each hour you contribute to the movement, they *earn* money every hour they work to maintain the status quo!

2. Set up accounts on all the social media platforms including the mainstream (for traffic) and the offbeat (to avoid deplatforming). I suggest you name your accounts Free the Children of [name of your state] or something like it. That way, each state's name can share the core term *Free the Children.*

3. Create a database of the Governor, all GOP state legislators, and all leading GOP Party officials. See the Appendix to get started.

4. Young Americans for Liberty has identified well over a hundred liberty-oriented state legislators, many of whom are in red states. See, https://yaliberty.org/door/. Make it a priority to contact those in your state and ask them to take the lead on this issue.

5. Form a statewide group with a chapter in each county; prepare a platform, form letters and flyers.

6. Draft proposed legislation and constitutional amendments. A volunteer lawyer could be very

helpful here. Simple battle plans are the best. Do not make it too complex as the state legislature itself has a staff filled with bill drafters who can shape it up for passage if they are on board with the movement.

7. Have a massive rally at the Capitol to announce the effort. Start lobbying the legislature that very day. Encourage members to flood their inboxes with letters and emails urging them to support repeal of compulsory socialist school laws.

8. Update the database as you get feedback, indicating whether each legislator supports us, opposes us or is undecided.

9. If they say, "No," publicly announce that you are seeking primary challengers against them in the next election and start to plan for those challenges.

10. If they say, "maybe," try to get their constituents to contact them to urge them to vote "Yes."

11. If your state has initiative and referenda, see Table 1 (Chapter 1), start organizing a petition drive. Don't wait to see whether the GOP will go along. "Fire all your guns at once."

12. After six months, you will know if the movement is catching on. Re-evaluate at that point. If the movement is stalling, then we will know that the GOP is, in fact, a complete fraud and hoax that should no longer be robotically supported but only when they actually deliver on their promises which is once in a dog's age.

13. Don't forget direct citizen action. Follow the protocol outlined in *Government Schools Are Bad for Your Kids:*

   • Pull your kids out of government schools.

   • Move to other states or counties to cut costs.[37]

---

[37] See, *LibertyMovement.org.*

- Find alternatives such as homeschooling.

Keep in mind that like-minded activists in 23 states will be working hard to accomplish the same goal. If progress does not happen in your state, consider voting with your feet and moving to a state that offers better educational choice and a lower cost of living. See Table 3, which lists the top eight red states by their degree of educational freedom.

Table 3

Red States Ranked by Degree of Education Choice

State	Rank/50
Arizona	1
Florida	2
Indiana	3
Georgia	4
New Hampshire	9
Oklahoma	11
Montana	13
Mississippi	15

Contact the Tenth Amendment Center for help on drafting legislation and lobbying. They have loads of experience advocating for bills to nullify federal laws at the state level and their skill set applies just as well to this effort.[38]

---

[38] *tenthamendmentcenter.com.*

What You Can Do to Light a Fire Under the GOP and Conservatism, Inc.

There are liberty-oriented think tanks in each red state. See the list below. Reach out to them for advice, research and contacts.

- Alabama: Alabama Policy Institute
- Arizona: Goldwater Institute
- Arkansas: Advance Arkansas Institute, Arkansas Policy Foundation
- Florida: Foundation for Government Accountability, James Madison Institute
- Georgia: Georgia Center for Opportunity, Georgia Public Policy Foundation
- Idaho: Idaho Freedom Foundation
- Indiana: Indiana Policy Review Foundation
- Iowa: Tax Education Foundation
- Mississippi: Empower Mississippi, Mississippi Center for Public Policy
- Missouri: Show-Me Institute
- Montana: Frontier Institute
- Nebraska: Platte Institute for Economic Research
- New Hampshire: Josiah Bartlett Center for Public Policy, Granite Institute
- North Dakota: Rough Rider Policy Center
- Ohio: Buckeye Institute
- Oklahoma: Oklahoma Council of Public Affairs
- South Carolina Palmetto Promise Institute
- South Dakota: Great Plains Public Policy Institute
- Tennessee: Beacon Center of Tennessee
- Texas: Texas Public Policy Foundation
- Utah: Libertas Institute, Sutherland Institute
- West Virginia: Cardinal Institute for West Virginia Policy
- Wyoming: Wyoming Liberty Group

Success is not guaranteed. You will likely face tremendous opposition and you will need to be prepared to counter-punch, using creative strategies and tactics. If the GOP, Conservative, Inc. and the establishment conservative media refuse to back this effort wholeheartedly, you need to respond in ways that get their attention.

What You Can Do to Light a Fire Under the GOP and Conservatism, Inc.

These organizations thrive on your *donations*, your *votes*, and your *patronage* of their TV and radio shows, magazines, websites and podcasts. If these groups refuse to support *you* on this key issue, and refuse to act in accordance with their own stated principles, the questions must be asked, why should you continue to support *them*? Vote for them? Give them your donations? Watch their shows? These questions answer themselves. But make your decision to withdraw support loudly and clearly. Let these organizations know that it was *their failure to truly support school choice* that is costing them your support.

Don't let them con you with the same old public relations tricks. Their classic ploy is to make you fear the Democratic bogeyman in the closet. I suggest you respond, "You Republicans act like closeted Democrats. You have failed and you need to be replaced by better people and better organizations. You are crowding out the ability of new and better people to come to fruition and actually defeat the Democratic bogeyman in the closet."

Conclusion

This is a critical time. America as we have known it may not survive much longer if present trends continue. A recent article[39] in the *New York Times*, entitled, "Is Civil War Coming to America," raises a prospect I alluded to in my *Progressivism: A Primer* in 2014:

> "The United States is not immune to the forces of history and the laws of economics. It too can and will vanish, most likely in an exceedingly unpleasant manner, if it continues on its present path."[40]

The country *did* in fact continue on its divisive and destructive path for eight more years, prompting the recent publication of two more books that warn of civil war, *How Civil Wars Start and How to Stop Them*, by Barbara F. Walter, and *The Next Civil War: Dispatches From the American Future*, by Stephen Marche.

Out of the three main causes of our radical shift to the progressive-left and the racial divisions and chaos in the streets that has caused—immigration, the left-wing takeover of colleges, and the left-progressive domination of K-12 government schools—*only the last factor is subject to the control of ordinary citizens right now in at least in 23 states*.

This book proposes a workable strategy to change our trajectory of steady decline towards left-wing totalitarianism and civil conflict. *If anyone has a better idea, please shout it from the mountaintops.*

This idea gives America a way out of its conundrum of how to avoid the steady road toward disaster and self-destruction. It also gives the GOP and Conservatism, Inc. a last chance at redemption *after decades of total failure* that have led us to our present debacle. Do not tarry!

---

[39] By Ian Bassin, January 18, 2022.
[40] *Progressivism: A Primer,* p. 196. This book also anticipated the racial unrest that was to come. See, pp. 17-18.

Conclusion

There is a tide in the affairs of men
Which, taken at the flood, leads on to fortune;
Omitted, all the voyage of their life
Is bound in shallows and in miseries.
On such a full sea are we now afloat;
And we must take the current when it serves,
Or lose our ventures."

— William Shakespeare, *Julius Caesar*

Appendix

Alabama

Population	4.9 million
Republican Voting Advantage[41]	R+15
Date of compulsory School law[42]	1915
Age mandates[43]	6-17
Educational freedom rank	23/50
—*Freedom in the Fifty States*	

Constitutional provisions to be repealed:

SECTION 256

Duty of legislature to establish and maintain public school system; apportionment of public school fund; separate schools for white and colored children.

The legislature shall establish, organize, and maintain a liberal system of public schools throughout the state for the benefit of the children thereof between the ages of seven and twenty-one years. The public school fund shall be apportioned to the several counties in proportion to the number of school children of school age therein, and shall be so apportioned to the schools in the districts or townships in the counties as to provide, as nearly as practicable, school terms of equal duration in such school districts or townships. Separate schools shall be provided for white and colored children,

---

41 Otherwise known as Partisan Voting Index. Source: worldpopulationreview.com

42 Source: *Wikipedia.*

43 Source: *need.ed.gov*

and no child of either race shall be permitted to attend a school of the other race.[44]

It is the policy of the state of Alabama to foster and promote the education of its citizens in a manner and extent consistent with its available resources, and the willingness and ability of the individual student, but nothing in this Constitution shall be construed as creating or recognizing any right to education or training at public expense, nor as limiting the authority and duty of the legislature, in furthering or providing for education, to require or impose conditions or procedures deemed necessary to the preservation of peace and order.

Statutory provisions to be repealed:

2006 Alabama Code - Section 16-28-3 — Ages of children required to attend school; church school students exempt from operation of this section.

Every child between the ages of seven and 16 years shall be required to attend a public school, private school, church school, or be instructed by a competent private tutor for the entire length of the school term in every scholastic year except that every child attending a church school as defined in Section 16-28-1 is exempt from the requirements of this section, provided such child complies with enrollment and reporting procedure specified in Section 16-28-7. Admission to public school shall be on an individual basis on the application of the parents, legal custodian or guardian of the child to the local board of education at the beginning of each school year, under such rules and regulations as the board may prescribe.

2006 Alabama Code - Section 16-28-12 — Person in loco parentis responsible for child's school attendance and behavior; noncompliance; local boards to promulgate written behavior policy, contents, annual distribution, receipt to be documented; school officials required to report noncompliance; failure to report

---

[44] Overruled by *Brown v. Board of Education*, 347 U. S. 483 (1954).

Appendix

suspected violation; district attorneys vigorously to enforce provisions.

(a) Each parent, guardian, or other person having control or custody of any child required to attend school or receive regular instruction by a private tutor who fails to have the child enrolled in school or who fails to send the child to school, or have him or her instructed by a private tutor during the time the child is required to attend a public school, private school, church school, denominational school, or parochial school, or be instructed by a private tutor, or fails to require the child to regularly attend the school or tutor, or fails to compel the child to properly conduct himself or herself as a pupil in any public school in accordance with the written policy on school behavior adopted by the local board of education pursuant to this section and documented by the appropriate school official which conduct may result in the suspension of the pupil, shall be guilty of a misdemeanor and, upon conviction, shall be fined not more than one hundred dollars ($100) and may also be sentenced to hard labor for the county for not more than 90 days. The absence of a child without the consent of the principal teacher of the public school he or she attends or should attend, or of the tutor who instructs or should instruct the child, shall be prima facie evidence of the violation of this section.

(b) Each local public board of education shall adopt a written policy for its standards on school behavior. Each local public school superintendent shall provide at the commencement of each academic year a copy of the written policy on school behavior to each parent, guardian, or other person having care or control of a child who is enrolled. Included in the written policy shall be a copy of this section. The signature of the student and the parent, guardian, or other person having control or custody of the child shall document receipt of the policy.

(c) Any parent, guardian, or other person having control or custody of any child enrolled in public school who fails to require the child to regularly attend the school or tutor, or fails to compel the child to properly conduct himself or herself as a pupil in accordance with the written policy on school behavior adopted by the local board of education and documented by the appropriate school official which conduct may result in the suspension of the pupil, shall be reported by the principal to the superintendent of education of the school system in which the suspected violation occurred. The superintendent of education or his or her designee shall report suspected violations to the district attorney within 10 days. Any principal or superintendent of education or his or her designee intentionally failing to report a suspected violation shall be guilty of a Class C misdemeanor. The district attorney shall vigorously enforce this section to ensure proper conduct and required attendance by any child enrolled in public school.

GOP Contact info:

John Wahl, Chairman

Email: john@algop.org

Find county GOP officials:

https://algop.org/our-party/find-local-gop/

Governor

Kay Ivey

https://contact.governor.alabama.gov/contact.aspx

State Legislature contacts

Speaker of the House

Mac McCutcheon

mac.mccutcheon@alhouse.gov

Appendix

Members

http://www.legislature.state.al.us/aliswww/ISD/House/ALRepresentatives.aspx

Majority Leader of the Senate

Clay Schofield

Clay.schofield@alsenate.gov

Members

http://www.legislature.state.al.us/aliswww/ISD/Senate/ALSenatorsbyDistrict.aspx

Appendix

Arizona

Population	7.1 million
Republican Voting Advantage	R+3
Date of compulsory School law	1899
Age mandates	6-16
Educational freedom rank	1/50

—*Freedom in the Fifty States*

Constitutional provisions to be repealed:

Section 1. A. The legislature shall enact such laws as shall provide for the establishment and maintenance of a general and uniform public school system, which system shall include:

1. Kindergarten schools.

2. Common schools.

3. High schools.

4. Normal schools.

5. Industrial schools.

Seventh. Provisions shall be made by law for the establishment and maintenance of a system of public schools which shall be open to all the children of the state and be free from sectarian control, and said schools shall always be conducted in English.

Appendix

Statutory provisions to be repealed:

15-802. School instruction; exceptions; violations; classification; definitions

A. Every child between the ages of six and sixteen years shall attend a school and shall be provided instruction in at least the subjects of reading, grammar, mathematics, social studies and science. The person who has custody of the child shall choose a public, private or charter school or a homeschool as defined in this section to provide instruction or shall sign a contract to participate in an Arizona empowerment scholarship account pursuant to section 15-2402.

****

E. Unless otherwise exempted in this section or section 15-803, a parent of a child between six and sixteen years of age or a person who has custody of a child, who does not provide instruction in a homeschool and who fails to enroll or fails to ensure that the child attends a public, private or charter school pursuant to this section or fails to sign a contract to participate in an empowerment scholarship account pursuant to section 15-2402 is guilty of a class 3 misdemeanor. A parent who fails to comply with the duty to file an affidavit of intent to provide instruction in a homeschool is guilty of a petty offense.

GOP Contact info:

Kelli Ward, Chair

kelli.ward@azgop.org

Find county GOP officials:

azgop.com/directory/county-parties

Appendix

Governor

Doug Duchy

azgovernor.gov

State Legislature contacts

Speaker of the House

Russell "Rusty" Bowers

Members—allege.com

Leader of the Senate

Karen Fann

FFann@azleg.gov

Members—allege.com

Appendix

Arkansas

Population	3.0 million
Republican Voting Advantage	R+16
Date of compulsory School law	1909
Age mandates	5-17
Educational freedom rank	25/50

—Freedom in the Fifty States

Constitutional provisions to be repealed:

"Intelligence and virtue being the safeguards of liberty and the bulwark of a free and good government, the State shall ever maintain a general, suitable and efficient system of free public schools and shall adopt all suitable means to secure to the people the advantages and opportunities of education." *Art. 14, section 1.*

Statutory provisions to be repealed:

"Under the penalty for noncompliance set by law, every parent, legal guardian, person having lawful control of the child, or person standing in loco parentis residing within the State of Arkansas and having custody or charge of a child five (5) years of age through seventeen (17) years of age on or before the date established in § 6-18-207 for the minimum age for enrollment in public school shall enroll and send the child to a public, private, or parochial school or provide a home school for the child. . . " Title 6. § 6-18-201.

GOP Contact info:

Jonelle Fulmer, Chairman

Communications@arkansasgop.org

Appendix

Find county GOP officials:

https://www.arkansasgop.org/countygop.html

Governor

Asa Hutchinson

Phone: (501) 682-2345

State Legislature contacts

Speaker of the House

Matthew J. Shepherd
matthew.shepherd@arkansashouse.org

Members

https://www.arkansashouse.org/representatives/members

Majority Leader of the Senate

Scott Flip

scott.Flippo@senate.ar.gov

Members

https://senate.arkansas.gov/senators/senator-search/

Appendix

Florida

Population	21.5 million
Republican Voting Advantage	R+3
Date of compulsory School law	1915
Age mandates	6-16
Educational freedom rank	2/50

—Freedom in the Fifty States

Constitutional provisions to be repealed:

"The education of children is a fundamental value of the people of the State of Florida. It is, therefore, a paramount duty of the state to make adequate provision for the education of all children residing within its borders. Adequate provision shall be made by law for a uniform, efficient, safe, secure, and high quality system of free public schools that allows students to obtain a high quality education and for the establishment, maintenance, and operation of institutions of higher learning and other public education programs that the needs of the people may require." *Article IX, Section 1(a).*

Statutory provisions to be repealed:

All children who have attained the age of 6 years or who will have attained the age of 6 years by February 1 of any school year or who are older than 6 years of age but who have not attained the age of 16 years, except as otherwise provided, are required to attend school regularly during the entire school term. XLVIII-1003.21(1)(a)1.

GOP Contact info:

Joe Gruters, Chairman

(850) 222-7920

Appendix

Find county GOP officials:

Florida.gop/reds

Governor

Ron DeSantis

(850) 717-9337

State Legislature contacts

Speaker of the House

Chris Sprowls

(850) 717-5000

Members

https://www.myfloridahouse.gov/representatives

President of the Senate

Wilton Simpson

(850) 487-5229

Members

https://www.flsenate.gov/Senators/Find

Appendix

Georgia

Population	10.7 million
Republican Voting Advantage	R+3
Date of compulsory School law	1916
Age mandates	6-16
Educational freedom rank	4/50

—*Freedom in the Fifty States*

Constitutional provisions to be repealed:

"Public education; free public education prior to college or postsecondary level; support by taxation. The provision of an adequate public education for the citizens shall be a primary obligation of the State of Georgia. Public education for the citizens prior to the college or postsecondary level shall be free and shall be provided for by taxation, and the General Assembly may by general law provide for the establishment of education policies for such public education. The expense of other public education shall be provided for in such manner and in such amount as may be provided by law." *Article VIII, Section 1.*

Statutory provisions to be repealed:

"Mandatory attendance in a public school, private school, or home school program shall be required for children between their sixth and sixteenth birthdays." *O.C.G.A. 20-2-690.1(a).*

GOP Contact info:

David Shafer, Chairman

404.257.5559

Appendix

Find county GOP officials:

https://gagop.org/about/

Governor

Brian Kemp

(404) 656-1776

State Legislature contacts

Speaker of the House

David Ralston

(404) 656-5020

Members

https://www.legis.ga.gov/members/house

Majority Leader of the Senate

Sen. Mike Dugan

404-656-7872

Members

https://www.legis.ga.gov/members/senate

Appendix

Idaho

Population	1.8 million
Republican Voting Advantage	R+19
Date of compulsory School law	1887
Age mandates	7-16
Educational freedom rank	27/50

—*Freedom in the Fifty States*

Constitutional provisions to be repealed:

The stability of a republican form of government depending mainly upon the intelligence of the people, it shall be the duty of the legislature of Idaho, to establish and maintain a general, uniform and thorough system of public, free common schools. Article IX, Section 1.

The legislature may require by law that every child shall attend the public schools of the state, throughout the period between the ages of six and eighteen years, unless educated by other means, as provided by law. Article IX, Section 9.

Statutory provisions to be repealed:

"The parent or guardian of any child resident in this state who has attained the age of seven (7) years at the time of the commencement of school in his district, but not the age of sixteen (16) years, shall cause the child to be instructed in subjects commonly and usually taught in the public schools of the state of Idaho. To accomplish this, a parent or guardian shall either cause the child to be privately instructed by, or at the direction of, his parent or guardian; or

Appendix

enrolled in a public school or public charter school, including an on-line or virtual charter school or private or parochial school during a period in each year equal to that in which the public schools are in session; there to conform to the attendance policies and regulations established by the board of trustees, or other governing body, operating the school attended." 33-202.

GOP Contact info:

Tom Luna, Chairman

(208) 343-6405

Find county GOP officials:

https://www.idgop.org/county-parties/

Governor

Brad Little

208-334-2100

State Legislature contacts

Speaker of the House

Scott Bedke (R)

SBedke@house.idaho.gov

Members

https://legislature.idaho.gov/house/membership/

Appendix

Majority Leader of the Senate

Kelly Arthur Anthon (R)

KAnthon@senate.idaho.gov

Members

https://legislature.idaho.gov/senate/membership/

Appendix

Indiana

Population	6.8 million
Republican Voting Advantage	R+11
Date of compulsory School law	1897
Age mandates	7-18
Educational freedom rank	3/50

—Freedom in the Fifty States

Constitutional provisions to be repealed:

"Knowledge and learning, generally diffused throughout a community, being essential to the preservation of a free government; it shall be the duty of the General Assembly to encourage, by all suitable means, moral, intellectual, scientific, and agricultural improvement; and to provide, by law, for a general and uniform system of Common Schools, wherein tuition shall be without charge, and equally open to all." Article 8, Section 1.

Statutory provisions to be repealed:

Subject to the specific exceptions under this chapter, a Indiana Code 2015—student shall attend either:

(1) a public school that the student is entitled to attend under IC 20-26-11; or (2) another school taught in the English language. IC 20-33-2-4.

GOP Contact info:

Kyle Hupfer, Chairman

317-635-7561

Appendix

Find county GOP officials:

http://indiana.gop/counties

Governor

Eric J. Holcomb

317-232-4567

State Legislature contacts

Speaker of the House

Todd Huston

317-232-9677

Members

http://iga.in.gov/legislative/find-legislators/

Leader of the Senate

Rodric Bray

Senator.Bray@iga.in.gov

Members

http://iga.in.gov/legislative/find-legislators/

Appendix

Iowa

Population	3.2 million
Republican Voting Advantage	R+6
Date of compulsory School law	1902
Age mandates	6-16
Educational freedom rank	18/50
—Freedom in the Fifty States	

Constitutional provisions to be repealed:

The Board of Education shall provide for the education of all the youths of the State, through a system of Common Schools and such school shall be organized and kept in each school district at least three months in each year. Any district failing, for two consecutive years, to organize and keep up a school as aforesaid may be deprived of their portion of the school fund. Article IX, Section 12.

Statutory provisions to be repealed:

Except as provided in section 299.2, the parent, guardian, or legal or actual custodian of a child who is of compulsory attendance age shall cause the child to attend some public school or an accredited nonpublic school, or place the child under competent private instruction or independent private instruction in accordance with the provisions of chapter 299A, during a school year, as defined under section 279.10. 299.1

Appendix

GOP Contact info:

Jeff Kaufmann, Chairman

(515) 282-8105

Governor

Kim Reynolds

(515) 281-5211

State Legislature contacts

Speaker of the House

Pat Grassley

pat.grassley@legis.iowa.gov

Members

https://www.legis.iowa.gov/legislators/house

Majority Leader of the Senate

Jack Whitver

jack.whitver@legis.gov

Members

https://www.legis.iowa.gov/legislators/senate

Appendix

Mississippi

Population	2.9 million
Republican Voting Advantage	R+9
Date of compulsory School law	1918
Age mandates	6-17
Educational freedom rank	16/50

—Freedom in the Fifty States

Constitutional provisions to be repealed:

"The Legislature shall, by general law, provide for the establishment, maintenance and support of free public schools upon such conditions and limitations as the Legislature may prescribe." Art. 8, Section 201.

Statutory provisions to be repealed:

"A parent, guardian or custodian of a compulsory-school-age child in this state shall cause the child to enroll in and attend a public school or legitimate nonpublic school for the period of time that the child is of compulsory school age, except under the following circumstances. . ." § 37-13-91(3).

GOP Contact info:

Frank Bordeaux, Chairman

601-948-5191

Appendix

Governor

Tate Reeves

governor@govreeves.ms.gov.

State Legislature contacts

Speaker of the House

Philip Gunn

(601)359-3300

Members

http://www.legislature.ms.gov/legislators/representatives/

Leader of the Senate

Dean Kirby

(601) 359-4089

Members

http://www.legislature.ms.gov/legislators/senators/

Appendix

Missouri

Population	6.1 million
Republican Voting Advantage	R+10
Date of compulsory School law	1905
Age mandates	7-17
Educational freedom rank	30/50

—Freedom in the Fifty States

Constitutional provisions to be repealed:

A general diffusion of knowledge and intelligence being essential to the preservation of the rights and liberties of the people, the general assembly shall establish and maintain free public schools for the gratuitous instruction of all persons in this state within ages not in excess of twenty-one years as prescribed by law. Art. XI, Sec. 1.

Statutory provisions to be repealed:

167.031. School attendance compulsory, who may be excused — nonattendance, penalty — home school, definition, requirements — school year defined — daily log, defense to prosecution — compulsory attendance age for the district defined. — 1. Every parent, guardian or other person in this state having charge, control or custody of a child not enrolled in a public, private, parochial, parish school or full-time equivalent attendance in a combination of such schools and between the ages of seven years and the compulsory attendance age for the district is responsible for enrolling the child in a program of academic instruction which complies with subsection 2 of this section. Any parent, guardian or other person who enrolls a child between the ages of five and seven years in a public school program of academic instruction shall cause such child to attend the academic program on a regular basis, according to this section. Nonattendance by such child shall cause such parent, guardian or other responsible person to be in violation of the provisions of section 167.061, except as provided by this section. A parent, guardian or other person in this state having charge, control, or custody of a child between the ages of seven years of age and the compulsory attendance age for the district shall cause the child to attend regularly some public, private, parochial, parish, home school or a combination of such schools not less than the entire school term of the school which the child attends . . .

GOP Contact info:

Chairman

Nick Myers

chairman@mogop.org

Find county GOP officials:

https://missouri.gop/wp-content/uploads/2019/02/County-Chairs-2019-2020.pdf

Governor

Michael Parson

(573) 751-3222

Appendix

State Legislature contacts

Speaker of the House

Rob Verscovo

Rob.verscovo@house.mo.gov

Members

https://house.mo.gov

Majority Leader of the Senate

Caleb Rowden

(573) 751-3931

Members

https://www.senate.mo.gov/senators-listing/

Appendix

Montana

Population	1.1 million
Republican Voting Advantage	R+11
Date of compulsory School law	1883
Age mandates	7-16
Educational freedom rank	14/50

—*Freedom in the Fifty States*

Constitutional provisions to be repealed:

Part X. EDUCATION AND PUBLIC LANDS

"The legislature shall provide a basic system of free quality public elementary and secondary schools. The legislature may provide such other educational institutions, public libraries, and educational programs as it deems desirable. It shall fund and distribute in an equitable manner to the school districts the state's share of the cost of the basic elementary and secondary school system. Part X, Section 1(3).

Statutory provisions to be repealed:

"Except as provided in subsection (2), any parent, guardian, or other person who is responsible for the care of any child who is 7 years of age or older prior to the first day of school in any school fiscal year shall cause the child to be instructed in the program prescribed by the board of public education pursuant to 20-7-111 until the later of the following dates:
(a) the child's 16th birthday; or

(b) the date of completion of the work of the 8th grade." MT Code § 20-5-102.

GOP Contact info:

Don Kaltschmidt, Chairman

406.442.6469

Governor

Greg Pianoforte

406-444-3111

State Legislature contacts

Speaker of the House

Wylie Galt

406.220.0157

Members

https://leg.mt.gov/map/

Majority Leader of the Senate

Cary Smith

cary.smith@mtleg.gov

Members

https://leg.mt.gov/map/

Appendix

Nebraska

Population	1.9 million
Republican Voting Advantage	R+13
Date of compulsory School law	1887
Age mandates	6-18
Educational freedom rank	47/50

—*Freedom in the Fifty States*

Constitutional provisions to be repealed:

"The Legislature shall provide for the free instruction in the common schools of this state of all persons between the ages of five and twenty-one years. The Legislature may provide for the education of other persons in educational institutions owned and controlled by the state or a political subdivision thereof." Article VII-1

Statutory provisions to be repealed:

For purposes of this section, a child is of mandatory attendance age if the child (a) will reach six years of age prior to January 1 of the then-current school year and (b) has not reached eighteen years of age. 79-201(1).

GOP Contact info:

Dan Welch, Chairman

(402) 475-2122

Appendix

Find county GOP officials:

https://www.ne.gop/localgop

Governor

Pete Ricketts

(402) 471-2244

State Legislature contacts

Speaker of the Legislature

Mike Hilgers

mhilgers@leg.ne.gov

Members

https://nebraskalegislature.gov/senators/senator_list.php

New Hampshire

Population	1.4 million
Republican Voting Advantage	R+0
Date of compulsory School law	1871
Age mandates	6-18
Educational freedom rank	5/50

—*Freedom in the Fifty States*

Statutory provisions to be repealed:

"A parent of any child at least 6 years of age and under 18 years of age shall cause such child to attend the public school to which the child is assigned in the child's resident district. Such child shall attend full time when such school is in session unless. . . " 15-193:1

GOP Contact info:

Stephen Stepanek, Chairman

603-225-9341

Find county GOP officials:

https://www.nh.gov/about

Appendix

Governor

Chris Sununu

(603) 271-2121

State Legislature contacts

Speaker of the House

Sherman Packard

sherman.packard@leg.state.nh.us

Members

http://www.gencourt.state.nh.us/house/members/

Majority Leader of the Senate

Jeb Bradley

Jeb.Bradley@leg.state.nh.us

Members

http://gencourt.state.nh.us/senate/members/senate_roster.aspx

Appendix

North Dakota

Population	779,000
Republican Voting Advantage	R+20
Date of compulsory School law	1883
Age mandates	7-16
Educational freedom rank	50/50

—*Freedom in the Fifty States*

Constitutional provisions to be repealed:

"The legislative assembly shall provide for a uniform system of free public schools throughout the state, beginning with the primary and extending through all grades up to and including schools of higher education, except that the legislative assembly may authorize tuition, fees and service charges to assist in the financing of public schools of higher education." Article XIII, Section 2.

Statutory provisions to be repealed:

"Any person having responsibility for a child between the ages of seven and sixteen years shall ensure the child attends a public school for the duration of each school year." 15.1-20-01.

GOP Contact info:

Perrie Schafer, Chairman

perrie@ndgop.org

Appendix

Find county GOP officials:

https://ndgop.org/state-committee/

Governor

Doug Burgum

701.328.2200

State Legislature contacts

Speaker of the House

Bill Devlin

bdevlin@nd.gov

Members

https://www.legis.nd.gov/assembly/67-2021/members/house

Majority Leader of the Senate

Rich Warren

701-483-6918

Members

https://www.legis.nd.gov/assembly/67-2021/members/senate

Appendix

Ohio

Population	11.8 million
Republican Voting Advantage	R+6
Date of compulsory School law	1877
Age mandates	6-18
Educational freedom rank	17/50

—Freedom in the Fifty States

Constitutional provisions to be repealed:

"The General Assembly shall make such provisions, by taxation, or otherwise, as, with the income arising from the school trust fund, will secure a thorough and efficient system of common schools throughout the state; but no religious or other sect, or sects, shall ever have any exclusive right to, or control of, any part of the school funds of this state." Article VI, Section 2.

Statutory provisions to be repealed:

"A child between six and eighteen years of age is "of compulsory school age" for the purpose of sections 3321.01 to 3321.13 of the Revised Code. A child under six years of age who has been enrolled in kindergarten also shall be considered "of compulsory school age" for the purpose of sections 3321.01 to 3321.13 of the Revised Code . . ." Title 33, Section 3321.01

Appendix

GOP Contact info:

Robert Paduchik, Chairman

(614) 228-2481

Governor

Mike DeWine

(614) 466-3555

State Legislature contacts

Speaker of the House

Robert R. Cupp

(614) 466-9624

Members

https://ohiohouse.gov/members/directory

Majority Leader of the Senate

Kirk Schuring

(614) 466-0626

Members

https://www.legislature.ohio.gov/legislators/senate-directory

Appendix

Oklahoma

Population	4.0 million
Republican Voting Advantage	R+20
Date of compulsory School law	1907
Age mandates	5-18
Educational freedom rank	11/50

—Freedom in the Fifty States

Constitutional provisions to be repealed:

"The Legislature shall establish and maintain a system of free public schools wherein all the children of the State may be educated." Section XIII-1.

"The Legislature shall provide for the compulsory attendance at some public or other school, unless other means of education are provided, of all the children in the State who are sound in mind and body, between the ages of eight and sixteen years, for at least three months in each year." Art. XIII-4.

Statutory provisions to be repealed:

It shall be unlawful for a parent, guardian, or other person having custody of a child who is over the age of five (5) years, and under the age of eighteen (18) years, to neglect or refuse to cause or compel such child to attend and comply with the rules of some public, private or other school, unless other means of education are provided for the full term the schools of the district are in session or the child is excused as provided in this section. § 70-10-105(A).

Appendix

GOP Contact info:

John Bennett, Chairman

(405) 528-3501

Find county GOP officials:

https://okgop.com/county-directory/

Governor

J. Kevin State

405.521.2342

State Legislature contacts

Speaker of the House

Charles McCall

(405) 557-7412

Members

https://www.okhouse.gov/MEMBERS/Default.aspx

Majority Leader of the Senate

Greg McCortney

(405) 521-5541

Members

https://oksenate.gov/senators

Appendix

South Carolina

Population	5.1 million
Republican Voting Advantage	R+8
Date of compulsory School law	1915
Age mandates	5-17
Educational freedom rank	19/50

—*Freedom in the Fifty States*

Constitutional provisions to be repealed:

"The General Assembly shall provide for the maintenance and support of a system of free public schools open to all children in the State and shall establish, organize and support such other public institutions of learning, as may be desirable." Article XI, Section 3.

Statutory provisions to be repealed:

A parent or guardian shall require his child to attend regularly a public or private school or kindergarten of this State which has been approved by the State Board of Education, a member school of the South Carolina Independent Schools' Association, a member school of the South Carolina Association of Christian Schools, or some similar organization, or a parochial, denominational, or church-related school, or other programs which have been approved by the State Board of Education from the school year in which the child is five years of age before September first until the child attains his seventeenth birthday or graduates from high school. A parent or guardian whose child is not six years of age on or before the first day of September of a particular school year may elect for their child or ward not to attend kindergarten. For this purpose, the parent or guardian shall sign a written document making the election with the governing body of the school district in which the parent or guardian resides. The form of this written document must be prescribed by regulation of the Department of Education. Upon the written election being executed, that child is not required to attend kindergarten. Section 59-65-10(A).

GOP Contact info:

Drew McKissick, Chairman

(803) 988-8440

Governor

Henry McMaster

803.734.2100

State Legislature contacts

Speaker of the House

James H. "Jay" Lucas

(803) 734-3125

Members

https://www.scstatehouse.gov/legislatorssearch.php

Appendix

Majority Leader of the Senate

A. Shane Massey

(803) 212-6330

Members

https://www.scstatehouse.gov/legislatorssearch.php

Appendix

South Dakota

Population	886,000
Republican Voting Advantage	R+16
Date of compulsory School law	1883
Age mandates	6-18
Educational freedom rank	24/50

—*Freedom in the Fifty States*

Constitutional provisions to be repealed:

Art. VIII, § 1. Uniform system of free public schools. The stability of a republican form of government depending on the morality and intelligence of the people, it shall be the duty of the Legislature to establish and maintain a general and uniform system of public schools wherein tuition shall be without charge, and equally open to all; and to adopt all suitable means to secure to the people the advantages and opportunities of education.

Statutory provisions to be repealed:

"Any person having control of a child of compulsory school age who fails to have the child attend school, as required by the provisions of this title, or provide alternative instruction pursuant to § 13-27-3, is guilty of a Class 2 misdemeanor for the first offense. For each subsequent offense, a violator of this section is guilty of a Class 1 misdemeanor." § 13-27-11

GOP Contact info:

Dan Lederman, Chairman

dan@southdakotagop.com

Appendix

Find county GOP officials:

Sdgop.com

Governor

Kristi Noem

605.773.3212

State Legislature contacts

Speaker of the House

Spencer Gosch

https://sdlegislature.gov/Legislators/Contacts/64

Members

https://sdlegislature.gov/Legislators/Contacts/64

Majority Leader of the Senate

Gary Cammack

Gary.Cammack@sdlegislature.gov

Members

https://sdlegislature.gov/Legislators/Contacts/64

Appendix

Tennessee

Population	6.9 million
Republican Voting Advantage	R+14
Date of compulsory School law	1905
Age mandates	6-18
Educational freedom rank	28/50

—Freedom in the Fifty States

Constitutional provisions to be repealed:

"The state of Tennessee recognizes the inherent value of education and encourages its support. The General Assembly shall provide for the maintenance, support and eligibility standards of a system of free public schools. The General Assembly may establish and support such post-secondary educational institutions, including public institutions of higher learning, as it determines." Article XI; Section 12.

Statutory provisions to be repealed:

"The public schools shall be free to all persons residing within the state who are above five (5) years of age or who will become five (5) years of age on or before August 31 for the 2013-2014 school year and on or before August 15 for all school years thereafter." Education § 49-6-3001(a)."

"Every parent, guardian or other legal custodian residing within this state having control or charge of any child or children between six (6) years of age and seventeen (17) years of age, both inclusive, shall cause the child or children to attend public or nonpublic school, and in event of failure to do so, shall be subject to the penalties provided in this part. Education § 49-6-3001(c)(1)."

Appendix

GOP Contact info:

Scott Golden, Chairman

golden@tngop.org

Find county GOP officials:

Tngop.org/find-local-gop

Governor

Bill Lee

(615) 741-2001

State Legislature contacts

Speaker of the House

Cameron Sexton

(615) 741-2343

Members

https://www.capitol.tn.gov/house/members/

Majority Leader of the Senate

Jack Johnson

(615) 741-2495

Members

https://www.capitol.tn.gov/senate/members/

Appendix

Texas

Population	29.1 million
Republican Voting Advantage	R+5
Date of compulsory School law	1915
Age mandates	6-19
Educational freedom rank	33/50

—Freedom in the Fifty States

Constitutional provisions to be repealed:

ARTICLE 7. EDUCATION

"A general diffusion of knowledge being essential to the preservation of the liberties and rights of the people, it shall be the duty of the Legislature of the State to establish and make suitable provision for the support and maintenance of an efficient system of public free schools." *Article 7, Section 1.*

Statutory provisions to be repealed:

"Unless specifically exempted by Section 25.086 (Exemptions), a child who is at least six years of age, or who is younger than six years of age and has previously been enrolled in first grade, and who has not yet reached the child's 19th birthday shall attend school." Sec. 25.085(b).

GOP Contact info:

Matt Rinaldi, Chairman

(512) 477-9821

Appendix

Find county GOP officials:

https://texasgop.org/county_chairs/

Governor

Greg Abbott

(512) 463-2000

State Legislature contacts

Speaker of the House

Dade Phelan

(409) 745-2777

Members

https://house.texas.gov/members/

Leader of the Senate

Dan Patrick (Lt. Gov)

(512) 463-5342

Members

https://www.senate.texas.gov/members.php

Appendix

Utah

Population	3.3 million
Republican Voting Advantage	R+13
Date of compulsory School law	1890
Age mandates	6-18
Educational freedom rank	22/50

—Freedom in the Fifty States

Constitutional provisions to be repealed:

"The Legislature shall provide for the establishment and maintenance of the state's education systems including: (a) a public education system, which shall be open to all children of the state; and (b) a higher education system. Both systems shall be free from sectarian control." Article X, Section 1

Statutory provisions to be repealed:

"Except as provided in Section 53A-11-102 or 53A-11-102.5, the parent of a school-age minor shall enroll and send the school-age minor to a public or regularly established private school." *53A-11-101.5(2).*

GOP Contact info:

Carson Jorgensen, Chairman

(801) 533-9777

Appendix

Governor

Spencer J. Cox

801-538-1000

State Legislature contacts

Speaker of the House

Brad Wilson

bradwilson@le.utah.gov

Members

https://house.utah.gov/house-members/

Majority Leader of the Senate

Evan J. Vickers

evickers@le.utah.gov

Members

https://senate.utah.gov/senate-roster/

Appendix

West Virginia

Population	1.8 million
Republican Voting Advantage	R+23
Date of compulsory School law	1897
Age mandates	6-17
Educational freedom rank	40/50
—Freedom in the Fifty States	

Constitutional provisions to be repealed:

1. The Legislature shall provide, by general law, for a thorough and efficient system of free schools. Article XII(1).

Statutory provisions to be repealed:

"Compulsory school attendance begins with the school year in which the sixth birthday is reached prior to July 1 of such year or upon enrolling in a full-time publicly funded kindergarten program, and continues to the 17th birthday or for as long as the student continues to be enrolled in a school system after the 17th birthday." *§18-8-1a.*

GOP Contact info:

Mark Harris, Chairman

mharris@wvgop.org

Appendix

Find county GOP officials:

wvgop.org/about-us/find-your-local-gop/

Governor

Jim Justice

304.558.2000

State Legislature contacts

Speaker of the House

Roger Hanshaw

roger.hanshaw@wvhouse.gov

Members

https://www.wvlegislature.gov/House/roster.cfm

President of the Senate

Craig Blair

craig.blair@wvsenate.gov

Members

www.wvlegislature.gov/Senate1/roster.cfm

Appendix

Wyoming

Population	576,000
Republican Voting Advantage	R+26
Date of compulsory School law	1876
Age mandates	7-16
Educational freedom rank	44/50

—*Freedom in the Fifty States*

Constitutional provisions to be repealed:

Art. 7, § 1. The legislature shall provide for the establishment and maintenance of a complete and uniform system of public instruction, embracing free elementary schools of every needed kind and grade, a university with such technical and professional departments as the public good may require and the means of the state allow, and such other institutions as may be necessary.

Statutory provisions to be repealed:

Title 21. Education § 21-4-102.

(a) Every parent, guardian or other person having control or charge of any child who is a resident of this state and whose seventh birthday falls on or before August 1, or September 15 if the child started kindergarten pursuant to an approved request under W.S. 21-3-110(a) (xxxviii), of any year and who has not yet attained his sixteenth birthday or completed the tenth grade shall be required to send such child to, and such child shall be required to attend, a public or private school each year, during the entire time that the public schools shall be in session in the district in which the pupil resides; provided, that the board of trustees of each school district may exempt any child from the operation of this article when:

Appendix

(i) The board believes that compulsory attendance in school would be detrimental to the mental or physical health of such child or the other children in the school; provided, the board may designate at the expense of the district a medical doctor of its choice to guide it and support it in its decision;

(ii) The board feels that compulsory school attendance might work undue hardship. The board may conduct a hearing on issues pursuant to this paragraph by executive session; or

(iii) The child has been legally excluded from the regular schools pursuant to the provisions of W. S. 21-4-306.

(b) A home-based educational program shall meet the requirements of a basic academic educational program pursuant to W. S. 21-4-101(a)(vi). It shall be the responsibility of every person administering a home-based educational program to submit a curriculum to the local board of trustees each year showing that the program complies with the requirements of this subsection. Failure to submit a curriculum showing compliance is prima facie evidence that the home-based educational program does not meet the requirements of this article.

(c) In addition to subsection (a) of this section, the parent, guardian or other person having control or charge of any child under the age of eighteen (18), who has not otherwise notified the district of enrolling that child in a different school district or in a private school or home-based educational program, shall meet in person with a school district counselor or administrator to provide the school district with written consent to the withdrawal of that child from school attendance. The written consent to withdrawal shall include a separate provision authorizing the release of the student's identity and address to the Wyoming national guard youth challenge program, as established by W. S. 19-9-701, for the sole purpose of recruitment into the Wyoming national guard youth challenge program.

Appendix

Title 21. Education § 21-4-104.

(a) Subject to the policy of the board of trustees, it shall be the duty of each attendance officer to:

(i) Counsel with students, parents, guardians or custodians and teachers; and to investigate the causes of unexcused absences;

(ii) Give written notice to the parent, guardian, or custodian of any child having an unexcused absence that the attendance of such child at school is required by law. If after such notice has been given, the child has a second unexcused absence, which the attendance officer reasonably believes was due to the willful neglect or failure of the parent, guardian, or custodian of the child, then he shall make and file a complaint against such parent, guardian, or custodian of such child before the district court for the violation of W. S. 21-4-102.

Title 21. Education § 21-4-105.

Any parent, guardian or custodian of any child to whom this article applies who willfully fails, neglects, or refuses to comply with the provisions of this article shall be guilty of a misdemeanor and shall be punished by a fine of not less than five dollars ($5.00) nor more than twenty-five dollars ($25.00) or by imprisonment in the county jail not more than ten (10) days or by both such fine and imprisonment.

GOP Contact info:

W. Frank Eathorne, Chairman

(307) 234-9166

Find county GOP officials:

https://www.wyoming.gop/county-parties

Appendix

Governor

Mark Gordon

Chief of Staff

buck.mcveigh@wyo.gov

State Legislature contacts

Speaker of the House

Eric Barlow

Eric.Barlow@wyoleg.gov

Members

Majority Leader of the Senate

Ogden Driskill

ogden.Driskill@wyoleg.gov

Members

https://www.wyoleg.gov/Legislators

Index

Index

Index

Other Books by James Ostrowski

Progressivism: A Primer on the Idea Destroying America

The Second Amendment Works!: A Primer on How to Defend Our Most Important Right

Direct Citizen Action: How We Can Win the Second American Revolution Without Firing a Shot

How We Can Revive the Liberty Movement and Defeat the Progressive State of America

The Impeachment of Barack Obama and Hillary Clinton: For High Crimes in Syria and Libya

Government Schools Are Bad for Your Kids: What You Need to Know

Political Class Dismissed: Essays Against Politics, Including "What's Wrong With Buffalo"

The Libertarian Devil's Dictionary

A Crime Against Humanity: Essays Against the Lockdown

About the Author

James Ostrowski is a trial and appellate lawyer and author from Buffalo, New York. He graduated from St. Joseph's Collegiate Institute in 1975 and obtained a degree in philosophy from the State University of New York at Buffalo in 1980. He graduated from Brooklyn Law School in 1983. In law school, he was writing assistant to Dean David G. Trager, later a federal judge in the Eastern District of New York. He was a member of the Moot Court Honor Society and the International Law Moot Court Team.

In 1984, he attended Murray Rothbard's private seminar on the History of Economic Thought in Manhattan.

He served as vice-chairman of the law reform committee of the New York County Lawyers Association (1986-88) and wrote two widely quoted reports critical of the law enforcement approach to the drug problem.

He was chair of the human rights committee, Erie County Bar Association (1997-1999). He has written a number of scholarly articles on the law on subjects ranging from drug policy to the commerce clause of the constitution.

His articles have appeared in the Wall Street Journal, Buffalo News, Cleveland Plain Dealer and Legislative Gazette. His policy studies have been published by the Hoover Institution, the Ludwig von Mises Institute, and the Cato Institute.

He is the author of *Government Schools Are Bad for Your Kids* (2009), *Direct Citizen Action* (2010), *Progressivism: A Primer* (2014) and *The Second Amendment Works* (2020).

He and his wife Amy live in North Buffalo and have two children. He was a long-time youth baseball and basketball coach. His hobbies include chess and hiking.

Made in the USA
Middletown, DE
18 March 2022

62704531R00068